Catholic Commentary on Ezra

INTRODUCTION

This Book take its name from the writer, who was a holy priest and doctor of the law. He is called by the Hebrews Ezra, (Challoner) and was son, (Tirinus) or rather, unless he lived above 150 years, a descendant of Saraias, 4 Kings xxv. 18. It is thought that he returned first with Zorobabel; and again, at the head of other captives, in the seventh year of Artaxerxes Longimanus, with ample authority. Esdras spent the latter part of his life in exhorting the people, and in explaining to them the law of God. He appeared with great dignity at the dedication of the walls of Jerusalem, 2 Esdras xii. 26, 35. We have four books which bear his name. (Calmet) --- This and the following book of Nehemias, originally made but one in Hebrew, (St. Jerome, &c.) as the transactions of both those great men are recorded. The third and fourth are not in Hebrew nor received into the canon of the Holy Scriptures, though the Greek Church hold the third as canonical, and place it first; (Worthington) and Genebrard would assert that both ought to be received, as they were by several Fathers. But they contain many things which appear to be erroneous, and have been rejected by others of great authority, and particularly by St. Jerome. The third book seems to have been written very early, by some Hellenist Jew, who was desirous of embellishing the history of Zorobabel; and the fourth was probably composed by some person of the same nation, who had been converted to Christianity, before the end of the second century; and who injudiciously attempted to convert his brethren, by assuming the name of a man who was so much respected. Many things have been falsely attributed to Esdras, on the same account. It is said that he invented the Masora; restored the Scriptures, which had been lost; fixed the canon of twenty-two books; substituted the Chaldaic characters instead of the ancient Hebrew, Samaritan, or Phoenician. But though Esdras might sanction the latter, now become common, the characters might vary insensibly, (Bianconi; Kennicott, Dis. ii.) as those of other languages have done, (Haydock) and the sacred books never perished wholly; nor could the canon be determined in the time of Esdras. (Calmet) --- As for the Masoretic observations and points, they are too modern an invention. (Elias Levita; Capel; Houbigant, &c.) --- What we know more positively of Esdras, is, (Worthington) that he was empowered by Artaxerxes to bring back the Jews, and that he acted with great zeal. (Haydock) --- This book contains the transactions of 82 years, till the year of the world 3550. The letter of Reum, and the king's answer, (chap. iv 7., till chap. vi. 19., and well as chap. vii. 12, 27) are in Chaldean; the rest of the work is in Hebrew. (Calmet) --- We may discover various mysteries concealed under the literal sense of this and the following book. (St. Jerome, ep. ad Paulin.) (Worthington) --- Esdras is supposed by this holy doctor, as well as by some of the Rabbins, &c., to have been the same person with the prophet Malachy [Malachias]; (Button) and several reasons seems to support this conjecture, though it must still remain very uncertain. (Calmet) --- Some think that (Haydock) Esdras wrote only the four last chapters and the author of Paralipomenon the six preceding ones. (Du Hamel) --- But it is most probable that he compiled both from authentic documents. (Haydock) --- Some few additions may have been inserted since, by divine authority, 2 Esdras xii. 11, 22. (Tirinus)

CHAPTER I

VERSE 1

In. Hebrew, "And (Calmet) or *But in,*" as [in] 2 Paralipomenon xxxvi. 22. (Haydock) --- Thus the historical works are connected. Spinosa infers, from this book being inserted after Daniel in the Hebrew Bible that the same author wrote both. But the order of the books in the Septuagint and Vulgate is far more natural, (Calmet) and this has often varied in Hebrew, &c. (Kennicott) See 2 Paralipomenon xxxvi. 23. (Haydock) --- *First.* The design was only put in execution the following year. (The year of the world 3468) --- *Cyrus* (Hebrew *coresh,* (Haydock) or Koresch) means "the sun," according to Ctesias and Plutarch. Josephus ([Antiquities] xi. 1.) inform us that this prince became a friend of the Jews, in consequence of having seen the prediction of Isaias (xliv. 28., and xlv. 1.) fulfilled in his own person. He took Babylon, the year of the world 3466, and established the Persian empire which was subverted by Alexander. (Calmet) --- he had before ruled over Persia 27 years, and only reigned three as sole monarch at Babylon. (Tirinus) --- *The Lord;* every good notion, even in infidels, proceeds from him. (Du Hamel) --- Cyrus was one of the best and greatest conquerors of antiquity. He was the son of Cambyses, by Mandane, princess of Media. Xenophon informs us that he died in his bed; (Haydock) and had been lately conquered. (Tirinus)

VERSE 2

Earth, which had belonged to the king of Babylon. (Haydock) --- This may be an hyperbole, or allusion to Isaias xlv. 1. (Menochius) --- The dominions of Cyrus were very extensive, (Xenophon, Cyrop. i. and viii.) reaching from Ethiopia to the Euxine sea, &c. He acknowledges that he received all from the hand of God. Nabuchodonosor makes a similar confession of his supreme dominion; (Daniel ii. 47) and the potentates of Egypt and of Rome, procured sacrifices to be offered to him. But what advantage did they derive from this sterile knowledge of his divinity since they did not honor him accordingly, but wished to join his worship with that of idols; though the force of miracles and of reason must have convinced them that there is but one God. (Calmet) --- *House,* or temple, Isaias xliv. 28. --- *Judea.* So the Septuagint read, but the Hebrew has "Juda," all along. The whole country now began to be know by the former name. (Haydock)

VERSE 3

He is the God, is placed within a parenthesis, by the Protestants. But the pagans might suppose that God was attached to this city, like their idols; and the temple was not yet begun. (Haydock)

VERSE 4

Rest, who do not please to return. The Jews went at different times, and under the different leaders, Zorobabel, Esdras, and Nehemias. Many did not return at all. Cyrus allowed them full liberty. He permits money to be exported, particularly the half sicle, required [in] Exodus xxx. 13, and all voluntary contributions for the temple. (Grotius) (Calmet) --- He also enjoins the prefects of the provinces, (ver. 6., and chap. iii. 7.) whom Josephus styles "the king's friends," to forward this work; and he even designed to perfect it at his own expense, chap. vi. 4.

VERSE 8

Gazabar means, "the treasurer." (Hebrew; Syriac; Calmet; Protestants; 3 Esdras ii. 19.) (Haydock) --- *Son* is not in Hebrew, &c., (Menochius) and must be omitted. (Tirinus) --- *Sassabasar.* This was another name for Zorobabel, (Challoner) given by the Chaldeans, as they changed the name of Daniel into Baltassar. (Eusebius, Præp. Evan. xi. 3.) (Tirinus) --- But others think that this was the Persian "governor (Junius) of Judea," (3 Esdras) as one reside at Jerusalem, till the days of Nehemias, 2 Esdras v. 14. It does not appear that Zorobabel was invested with this dignity, before the reign of Darius Hystaspes, Aggeus ii. 24. (Calmet)

VERSE 9

Knives. Septuagint, &c., "changes" of garments. (Calmet)

VERSE 10

Sort. Septuagint and Syriac, "double;" yet of less value. (Calmet) --- As no first sort had been mentioned, and some Latin manuscripts read 2410, agreeably to 3 Esdras ii. 12., and the truth, (Hallet) it may be inferred that "thousands were expressed anciently by single letters, with a dot over them." Afterwards, when numbers were expressed by words at length, the *b* being thus reduced to signify "two," was, of course, written *shnim;* but this word making nonsense with the following, has been changed into *mishnim,* a word not very agreeable to the sense here, and which leaves the sum total, now specified in the Hebrew text, very deficient for want of the 2000, thus omitted. (Kennicott, Dis. ii.) --- Josephus has, "30 golden cups, 2400 of silver." (Haydock)

VERSE 11

Hundred. Only 2499 are specified. 3 Esdras reads, 5469. Josephus ([Antiquities] xi. 1.) differs from all, reading 5210; which shews that the copies have varied, and that the Hebrew is incorrect. (Calmet) --- The use of number letters might cause this confusion. (Haydock) (Capel. iii. 20, 13.)

CHAPTER II

VERSE 1

Now. This catalogue is given again, 2 Esdras vii. 6., and 3 Esdras v. 7., immediately (Haydock) after the long interpolated story (Kennicott) of the three guards, concerning the superior strength of wine, the king, women or truth, in which Zorobabel gains the victory, in favor of the latter. (Haydock) --- The rest of the book is taken from other inspired writings; (Sandford) and this story may be borrowed Josephus: so that there is no reason for asserting "that one whole book is now lost out of the sacred canon." (Kennicott) --- Yet this argument is by no means conclusive, as the Paralipomenon consists of such supplements, &c. These three catalogues very considerably, not only in the proper names, but also in the numbers, (Haydock) though they must have been the same originally, and still give the same total, 42,360. We cannot find that number at present, by above 8,400. In many cases, the disagreement consists of a single unit, hundred, &c., which may lead us to suspect that the Palmyrene, or the more ancient Sidonian notation, may have been adopted in some Hebrew manuscripts, being used about the time of Christ. See Swinton's tables, (Phil. Trans. xlviii., and l.) where the Sidonian coins express the units by small perpendicular strokes; and the Palmyrene inscriptions only admit four of these together, having an arbitrary mark for 5: "the hundreds and units after the tens, are expressed in both, in the same manner as the single units." (Kennicott, 2 Diss.) --- Cordell (manuscript note on this author) disapproves of this mode of correcting, and says that the females are included in the total sum, being 12,542, not recorded in the separate sums. But this number seems too small, as there are generally as many of that sex as of the other. (Haydock) --- Some find the total 31,583, which leaves 10,777 wanting to complete 42,360, as these could not make out their genealogies, or were of the ten tribes. In this chapter only 29,818 are specified, whereas [in] 2 Esdras vii. has 31,089; the latter reckons 1765 unnoticed by Esdras, who has 494 not specified in Nehemias. The difference, that seems to make a reconciliation impossible, is what make these authors agree; for, if you add the surplus of each to the other, the same total, 31,583, will arise. (Alting. ep. 59.) This solution, though ingenious, is not solid or satisfactory. (Rondet, t. v. p. 176.) --- De Vence rather thinks that the difference is to be laid to the charge of transcribers, or that some people enrolled themselves after the registers had been made up; so that they are only included in the general sum. (Haydock) --- Some things may have been inserted from 2 Esdras, though here out of place, (Grotius) as we find similar anachronisms, 1 Paralipomenon ix. 2., and perhaps Genesis xxxvi. 31. Nehemias may also have included those whom he brought back along with these; unless we allow that someone, by attempting to reconcile the two, has thrown all into confusion. It seems undeniable, that some additions have been made to the latter book, chap. xii. 11, and 22. The list given [in] 1 Paralipomenon ix. 4., comprises only those who came first from Babylon. (Calmet) --- After this remark, it will hardly be requisite to specify all the variations of names and numbers. (Haydock) --- "For what can be hence inferred, but that there are some arithmetical mistakes in Scripture, which no one denies?" (Huet) --- "Almost all who are conversant with ancient copies, agree in the decision of St. Jerome, as they cannot but perceive that some variations have crept in, particularly with respect to numbers and proper names." (Walton) --- *Province,* born in Chaldea, (Menochius) or rather belonging to Judea, which was now considered as a province of the empire, (Calmet) and paid tribute, chap. iv. 13., and 2 Esdras ix. 36. (Tirinus) --- In 3 Esdras, we read, "These are they of Judea." --- *Nabuchodonosor* had taken some of these; the rest were chiefly their descendants. --- *Juda* now is used to denote Judea. (Haydock)

VERSE 2

Zorobabel was the prince, *Josue* the high priest. (Calmet) --- There are 12 mentioned in 2 and 3 Esdras. But here the sixth Nahamani, or Enenion, is omitted. (Haydock) --- There represent the 12 tribes, (Kennicott) and were chiefs. (Menochius) --- It is wonderful that Esdras is not here mentioned, as well as Nehemias, who led a company after him, many of whom are here recorded. (Calmet) --- They might come to take care of their patrimony, and return into Chaldea, like Mardochai, (Tirinus; though it does not seem to be Esther's uncle, Du Hamel) and Nehemias, who is styled also *Athersatha,* ver. 63. (Tirinus) ---*Baana.* 3 Esdras adds, "their leaders." (Haydock)

VERSE 3

Children. When this term precedes the name of a man, it means his offspring; (ver. 3, 20.) when placed before a city, it denotes the inhabitants, ver. 21, 35. (Calmet) --- The lay Israelites are placed here; then the Levitical tribe; (ver. 36.) the Nathineans, &c., ver. 43. It is very difficult to decide when the names designate places, and when persons. (Menochius)

VERSE 5

Seven. 2 Esdras, only 652. These arrived at Jerusalem; the rest altered their mind. (Junius) (Calmet) --- But 3 Esdras has 756: so that there is most probably a mistake somewhere. (Haydock)

VERSE 6

Moab. This seems to be the name of a place, where the descendants of Josue and Joab might reside; (chap. viii. 4.; Calmet) or *Phahath* might have this title, on account of some victory, or residence in the country. His descendants, with those of Josue and Joab, where 2812, (Tirinus) or 2818, 2 Esdras vii. 11. (Calmet) --- *Josue.* Protestants, "Jeshua *and* Joab." (Haydock) --- Some translate Pahath, "the chief of" Moab, &c. (Du Hamel) --- Grotius suspects that to ver. 68 may be inserted from Nehemias.

VERSE 13

Six. Other 60 returned afterwards with Esdras. (Haydock) (Chap. viii. 13.)

VERSE 16

Ather. 3 Esdras, Ator-Ezekios, 92: but 2 Esdras has *Ater, children of Hezecias,* 98. (Haydock)

VERSE 17

Besai. We should perhaps read Hasum, (ver. 19.; Calmet) then Besai, and afterwards *Jora,* who may be the same with Hareph, 2 Esdras vii. 24. (Haydock)

VERSE 20

Gebbar. 2 Esdras, *Gabaon.* 3 Esdras, "Baitereus, 3005." (Haydock)

VERSE 22

Six. 2 Esdras puts the inhabitants of those two cities together, and makes 188, instead of the present calculation 179. (Calmet) --- Netupha was in Ephraim. (Du Hamel)

VERSE 29

Nebo. 2 Esdras (vii. 33.) adds, "of the other Nebo," as in some Latin copies a first had been mentioned, (ver. 30.) where we have Geba, (Calmet) here written Gabaa, ver. 26. (Haydock) --- Nebo belonged to some of the other tribes, as well as Phahath-Moab; which shows that some of the people returned, (Calmet) and are particularized, as well as the men of the three tribes of Juda, Benjamin, and Levi. (Haydock)

VERSE 30

Megbis. 3 Esdras, "Niphis;" (Calmet) or, according to the Alexandrian Manuscript, "Phineis." (Haydock) --- The verse is omitted [in] 2 Esdras. But Megphias occurs below, chap. x. 20. Megabyse is a Persian name. (Herodotus iii. 20., and 160.)

VERSE 31

Other Elam. The first is mentioned (ver. 7.) with exactly the same number. Is not this verse redundant? (Calmet) --- Who would not be astonished? (Tirinus) --- 3 Esdras omits this and the following name. (Haydock)

VERSE 33

Hadid. These cities were in the tribe of Benjamin. (Calmet) --- *Senaa* was in Ephraim, eight miles from Jericho. (Eusebius)

VERSE 36

Josue, the high priest, ver. 2.

VERSE 40

Odovia, called Juda, chap. iii. 9. (Calmet)

VERSE 43

Nathinites, "people given" (1 Paralipomenon ix. 2.; Haydock) by Josue, David, and Solomon. (Tirinus)

VERSE 55

Servants, proselytes, 1 Paralipomenon xxii. 2. (Menochius)

VERSE 57

Pocereth-Hasebaim, in Hebrew (Calmet) or "of Zebaim." (Protestants)

VERSE 59

Thelmela, "the height of Mela, or of salt." The river Melas empties itself into the Euphrates. (Strabo xii.) --- The cities here mentioned were in Chaldea. Some of the ten tribes had probably been transported into Cappadocia, where Herodotus (ii. 35) place some circumcised Syrians. --- *Thelharsa,* or Thelassar, 4 Kings xix. 12. --- *Cherub,* &c., were cities of Chaldea, (Tirinus) or chief men, but as they had been carried away by Theglathphalassar, they had lost their genealogies, and could only produce circumcision as a proof that they were Israelites.

VERSE 61

Their name. The priest, Berzellai, assumed the name of the family, from which he had chosen a wife. (Haydock) --- It was that of the famous old man, who was so hospitable to David, 2 Kings xix. 31. (Calmet)

VERSE 62

Priesthood. Those who cannot prove that they are priests, ought not to exercise the functions. (Worthington) --- The Jews were particularly careful to preserve their genealogical tables, and transcribed them again after any very troublesome times. (Josephus, contra Apion 1, and in his own Life.) --- The Rabbins falsely assert that only the mother's side was examined, and that the children followed her condition. (Calmet)

VERSE 63

Athersatha. Protestants' marginal note, "the governor," (Haydock) in the Persian language. (Du Hamel) --- Nehemias had this title, 2 Esdras viii. 9. (Haydock) --- It means "a cup-bearer." (Calmet) (Menochius) --- 3 Esdras, "And Nehemias, *who is* also Atharias, said unto them, that they should not partake of the holy things, till a high priest, clothed with manifestation and truth, should arise." (Haydock) --- *Learned.* Hebrew, "with Urim and Thummim." We do not find that God had been consulted, in this manner, since the time of David: and the Jews inform us that the ornament was not used after the captivity, (Calmet) as it had been, perhaps, concealed with the ark, by Jeremias, 2 Machabees ii. 4. (Tirinus) --- Nehemias hoped that it would be soon recovered. In the mean time, he followed the spirit of the law, but with additional rigor, as it permitted such priests to eat consecrated meats, Leviticus xxi. 22. It seems that this decision is out of its proper place, since Nehemias came 80 years after Zorobabel. (Calmet) --- But he might have been present on this occasion, (Haydock) though he returned afterwards to Babylon, where he officiated as cup-bearer to the king. (Tirinus)

VERSE 64

Forty-two thousand, &c. Those who are reckoned up above of the tribes of Juda, Benjamin, and Levi, fall short of this number. The rest, who must be taken in to make up the whole sum, were of the other tribes. (Challoner) --- This explanation is given by R. Solomon. (Worthington) --- But we have seen that cities belonging to the ten tribes are specified. See ver. 1, and 29. (Haydock) --- Some might not be able to make out their genealogies, (Calmet) ver. 62. Yet some of these also are counted, ver. 60. (Haydock) --- The particular sums may therefore be incorrect. Josephus ([Antiquities] xi. 1) adds 102 to the number. (Calmet) --- 3 Esdras has, "But they were all of Israel from 12 years old and upwards, exclusive of boys and girls, (or male and female servants) 42,300." Grabe has in another character "sixty. The men and women servants of these, 7300." Then the Alexandrian Manuscript continues, "thirty-seven." So that without the addition it would give for the total, 42,337. Some copies (Haydock) have 40. (Calmet) --- But the most correct (Haydock) read 60. (Kennicott) The small number of servants and cattle show that the people were poor. (Du Hamel)

VERSE 65

Servants. Probably strangers. (Calmet) --- Yet the Hebrews might renounce their liberty, Exodus xxi. 6. (Haydock) --- *Hundred,* comprised in the last number; (Calmet) or they belong to Israel, but were different from those mentioned [in] ver. 41. We find 45 more in 2 and 3 Esdras. (Haydock) --- These might be inserted by Nehemias, after they had proved themselves to be of the tribe of Levi. (Tournemine) --- There were in all 49,942. (Haydock) So much was the power of this kingdom now reduced! Sulp Severus says above 50,000 of every sex and rank could not be found. (Haydock)

VERSE 69

Solids. Hebrew *darcemonim.* (Haydock) --- "Darics," worth as much as a golden sicle. (Pelletier) (Calmet) (1 Paralipomenon xxix. 7.) --- *Pounds,* (mnas) or 60 sicles. (Menochius) --- 3 Esdras has "mnas" in both places.

CHAPTER III

VERSE 1

Month. Tisri, famous for the feasts of trumpets, of expiation, and of tabernacles. (Du Hamel) --- The Israelites might spend four months on their journey, and two in making preparations for the feast of tabernacles, (Tirinus) and in erecting huts for themselves. (Calmet)

VERSE 2

Josue, or Jesus, (Jeshua) the son of Josedec: he was the high priest at that time; (Challoner) the first after the captivity. --- *Salathiel,* by whom he was brought up, though he was born of Phadaia, 1 Paralipomenon iii. 19. (Calmet) --- Protestants read Shealtiel.

VERSE 3

Fear. This must not prevent God's servants from offering sacrifice. (Worthington)

VERSE 7

Meat, in imitation of Solomon, 3 Kings v. 11. --- *Orders.* Hebrew, "permission." (Calmet) --- Protestants, "grant." (Haydock)

VERSE 8

Work. Hebrew adds, "of the house." Josias had appointed the Levites overseers, 2 Paralipomenon xxiv. 12. (Calmet)

VERSE 10

Hands; compositions, (Haydock) or ordinances. (Worthington) --- The 135th Psalm was sung, (Calmet) or the 117th. (Vatable)

VERSE 12

Temple. This second temple, though very large (2 Machabees xiv. 13.) and magnificent, (Aggeus ii. 10) never equaled the glory of the first, in its outward appearance, being also destitute of the ark, and perhaps of the Urim, &c. But the presence of the Messias gave it a more exalted dignity. (Calmet) --- *Joy.* These different emotions of grief and joy filled their breasts, (Du Hamel) thinking how they had brought on the judgments of God by their transgressions, and that he was now appeased, and would enable them to have some sort of a temple. (Tirinus) --- As it was less beautiful than that of Solomon, Aggeus must be understood to speak of the Church of Christ. (St. Augustine, de C. [City of God] xviii. 45.) (Worthington)

CHAPTER IV

VERSE 1

Enemies; Samaritans, and others, ver. 9.

VERSE 2

Asor Haddan sent a priest to instruct these people, but Salmanasar had transported them into the country. (Calmet) --- They continued for some time worshipping idols alone, and afterwards they consented to pay the like adoration to the Lord, 4 Kings xvii. 24, &c. (Haydock) --- It is clear, from their petition, that they had as yet no temple. The first was erected by them on Garizim, by leave of Alexander the Great, as a retreat for Manasses, brother of the Jewish high priest, and other who would not be separated from their strange wives. (Josephus, [Antiquities] xi.) --- Yet the Samaritan Chronicle, lately published, seems to give a higher antiquity to that temple, and pretends that a miracle declared in favor of the place. (Calmet) --- The fathers indeed adored there, (John iv. 20., and Genesis xii. 6) and Josue erected an altar on Hebal, but the Samaritan copy says it was to be on Garizim, Deuteronomy xxvii. 4., and Josue viii. 30. (Haydock)

VERSE 3

You, &c. Literally, "It is not for you and us to build." But why might not these people assist in the work, as well as king Hiram or Darius? (Haydock) --- Schematics and heretics must not communicate in sacrifices with Catholics, (Worthington) nor must the latter have society with them, in matters of religion. The Jews feared lest the Samaritans might introduce the worship of idols, or claim a part of the temple, or at least boast of what they had done. (Tirinus) --- They were aware of the insincerity of these people. (Menochius) --- The permission was moreover only granted to the Jews: (Calmet) but Cyrus had exhorted all to contribute; (chap. i. 4,) and Darius, as well as his pagan governors, were not repelled with disdain, chap. vi. 13. This treatment caused the Samaritans to be more inveterate, though the Jews were always more unwilling to come to a reconciliation. (Haydock) --- "For the Scripture did not say, the Samaritans have no commerce with the Jews," says St. Chrysostom in John iv. The Jewish authors inform us, that "Ezra, &c., gathered all the congregation into the temple, and the Levites sung and cursed the Samaritans,...that no Israelite eat of anything that is a Samaritan's, not that any Samaritan be proselyted to Israel, nor have any part in the resurrection," &c. (R. Tanchum)

(Lightfoot i. p. 598.) (Kennicott) --- If this were true, it would be carrying their resentment too far; as we ought to promote the conversion of the greatest reprobates. But we have no reason to condemn such great men. They knew the character of the Samaritans, and wished to bring them to a sense of their duty, by this rebuke. (Haydock)

VERSE 5

Counselors; ministers of the king, (Calmet) or governors of the provinces. (Tirinus) --- *Cyrus,* who was ignorant of their machination, (Josephus) being engaged in war with the Scythians. We may easily conceive what ill-disposed ministers may do, against the inclinations of their prince. (Calmet) --- *Darius,* son of Hystaspes, who succeeded the false Smerdis, after five months' usurpation. (Calmet)

VERSE 6

Assuerus; otherwise called Cambyses, the son and successor of Cyrus. He is also, in the following verse, named Artaxerxes, by a name common to almost all the kings of Persia, (Calmet) after Memnon. (Diodorus xv) Septuagint, "Arthasastha." *Arta* signifies "great," and *xerxes,* "warrior." (Herodotus vi. 98.) --- After Assuerus, some copies add, "he is Artaxerxes;" and Assuerus is so called in the Septuagint of Sixtus, 3 Esdras ii. 16. (Menochius)

VERSE 7

Artaxerxes may be the Oropastes of Trogus, (Calmet) or the false (Haydock) *Smerdis.* (Herodotus) ---*Beselam,* &c. These governed the provinces on the west side of the Euphrates. --- *Syriac* comprises the Chaldean, with which it as a great resemblance. It was spoken at the court of Babylon. (Xenophon vii.) See 4 Kings xviii. 26., and 2 Machabees xv. 37., and Daniel ii. 4.

VERSE 8

Beelteem. Syriac, "the son of Baltam." The term designates the office of Reum, "the master of reason," president of the council, treasurer, &c. (Calmet) --- Protestants, "chancellor." --- *From.* Protestants, "against." (Haydock) --- Hebrew, "concerning."

VERSE 9

Counselors. Septuagint and Syriac, "of our fellow-servants." Chaldean, "colleagues." This letter, and as far as chap. vi. 16, is in the Chaldean language. --- *Dinites,* perhaps the Denarenians. (Junius) (4 Kings xvii. 24.) (Calmet)

VERSE 10

Asenaphar, commonly supposed to be the Asarhaddon, though we know not that he caused any of these nations to remove thither, as Salmanasar certainly did. (Calmet) --- The name of the latter occurs in some copies. (Lyranus) --- *River,* Euphrates. --- *In peace.* (Haydock) --- The original, *cehenth,* is neglected by the Septuagint and Arabic. The Syriac reads, "Acheeneth." Others translate, "at that time," as if the date had been lost. (Junius, &c.) --- Protestants, "and at such a time." (Haydock) --- Others suppose the writers lived "at Kineeth." (Pagnin) --- But who ever heard of such a place? Le Clerc takes it to mean "and the rest," as if the title were curtailed. But it is more probable that the text ought to be Ceheth, as [in] ver. 17, and that we should translate, "beyond the river, (Calmet) *as now,* (11) unless this word ought to be here omitted, (Haydock) to Artaxerxes, the king, peace (and prosperity) as at present." (Calmet) --- Chaldean *sslum ucath,* "peace even now." (Haydock) --- So Horace says, *suaviter ut unc est,* wishing a continuation of happiness. 3 Esdras (ii. 17.) joins the last word with ver. 12, "And now be it," &c. *Canoth* may have this sense, (Calmet) and consequently no change is necessary. (Haydock)

VERSE 11

Him. This is a gloss. (Calmet) --- *Greeting.* Protestants, "and at such a time."

VERSE 12

Rebellious. The Jews had shown themselves impatient of subjection, contending with the kings of Assyria and Babylon, whose territories were now possessed by the successors of Cyrus, ver. 15. (Haydock)

VERSE 13

Revenues. Septuagint, &c., include all under the term of "tribute."

VERSE 14

Eaten. Chaldean, "on account of the salt, with which we have been salted, from the palace." The king's officers were fed from his table. Salt is put for all their emoluments; (Calmet) and hence the word *salary* is derived. (Pliny, [Natural History] xxxi. 7.) We may also translate, "because we have demolished the temple, and because," &c. (Kimchi; Grotius, &c.) But this seems to refined. (Calmet) --- Protestants, "Now because we have maintenance from *the king's* palace, and it is not meet," &c. To have neglected their master's interests, would have betrayed great ingratitude and perfidy; particularly if they had entered into a *covenant of salt*, or solemnly engaged to be ever faithful servants, as the nature of their office implied, Numbers xviii. 19., and 2 Paralipomenon xiii. 5. (Haydock) --- *Palace*, being honored with much distinction. (Delrio, adag. 215.)

VERSE 15

Fathers, the preceding emperors, Nabuchodonosor, Salmanasar, &c. (Haydock)

VERSE 16

Possession. Septuagint have simply, "peace."

VERSE 17

Greeting. Protestants, "peace, and at such a time," which has no great meaning. (Haydock) See ver. 10.

VERSE 19

Seditions: so are styled the just efforts of the Jews, to keep or to regain their liberty. (Calmet)

VERSE 20

Kings; only David and Solomon. (Menochius) --- They had made some on the east side of the river pay tribute, though the king may speak of the countries on the west.

VERSE 21

Hear. Chaldean, "give command," &c. --- *Further:* literally, "perhaps." (Haydock) --- This was a private edict, which might be rescinded, Daniel vi. 7.

VERSE 23

Beelteem, is not in Chaldean. --- *Arm*, or "force." (Protestants) (Haydock)

VERSE 24

House. They went beyond the order, which only forbade the building of the city, ver. 21. --- *Darius*, the year of the world 3485. (Calmet) --- He was the son of Hystaspes, (St. Jerome) and not Nothus, the sixth from Cyrus, as Sulpitius and Scaliger believe. (Tirinus)

CHAPTER V

VERSE 1

Addo was grand-father of the *prophet*, whose writings are extant. (Calmet) --- Both prophesied in the second year of Darius. (Menochius)

VERSE 2

Them. Aggeus had rebuked the people for building houses for themselves, while they neglected the temple. The work was hereupon resumed without any fresh order from the king; as the edicts of the usurper, Oropastes, were considered as null, and the Jews only answer the governor, that they had been authorized by Cyrus, ver. 13, 17. Josephus, and 3 Esdras iii., and iv. 47., assert that Darius had given leave. (Calmet) (Menochius)

VERSE 3

River, over all Syria, &c. This man had not been bribed, but acted with great moderation, and in compliance with his duty. (Calmet) --- *Counsel.* Chaldean, "order to make up this wall."

VERSE 4

In. Septuagint, "Then I (or they; *Greek: eipon.* The Syriac and Arabic declare for the latter) said thus to them: What," &c. --- *We gave.* Chaldean, "what are the names?" (Haydock) --- It seems Thathanai asked this question, ver. 10. The Jews might give in the names of Zorobabel, Josue, Aggeus, &c. (Calmet)

VERSE 5

Ancients. Septuagint, "captivity of Juda." (Haydock) --- Divine Providence favored the undertaking. (Delrio adag. 216.) (Menochius) (Psalm xxxii. 18.) --- His *eye* sometimes threatens ruin, Amos ix. 8. (Calmet) --- God did both on this occasion. (Worthington) --- *Hinder.* Chaldean, "cause them to leave off, till the matter came to Darius, (Haydock) and his decision was brought back;" (Calmet) or Protestants, "and then they returned answer by letter concerning this matter." Septuagint, "and they did not molest them, till the sentence should be brought to (or from) Darius; and then it (word) was sent to the tax-gatherer, concerning this *affair.*"

VERSE 8

Unpolished. Protestants, "great." (Haydock) --- Hebrew, "to be rolled." See Vitruv. x. 6. Septuagint, "choice stones." Kimchi, &c., "marble." (Calmet) --- 3 Esdras, "polished and precious stones." (Haydock) --- Yet the Vulgate seems more conformable to chap. vi. 4., and Aggeus ii. 2. (Menochius) (Ribera) ---*Walls*, every fourth course, 3 Kings vi. 36. (Calmet)

VERSE 13

Built. It did not appear that this edict had been revoked; (Calmet) nor could it be changed, if it had been passed by the advice of the Lord. (Haydock)

VERSE 14

Governor. Septuagint, "over the treasury."

VERSE 16

In building, being pretty far advanced, though for some time past it had been at a stand. (Haydock) --- It is not probable that Zorobabel said this, but the author of the letter added it, as he supposed the Jews continued to do some little. (Calmet) --- He desired to favor their cause, yet so as not to irritate the Samaritans. (Menochius)

CHAPTER VI

VERSE 1

Library. Protestants, "house of the rolls, where the treasures were," &c. ---*Babylon.* In the city, the search was fruitless: (Vatable) but in the kingdom, the record was discovered. (Menochius)

VERSE 2

Ecbatana. Chaldean *achmetha,* signifies "a jug, *or* chest." (Calmet) --- "They found in the chest of the palace, under the inscription of Media." (Munster) (Pagnin) --- "And a roll was found (some add, *in Amatha*) in the city, in a chest, (or tower; *Greek: Barei*) and this memorial was written in it." (Septuagint) Protestants style the place, "Achmetha." (Haydock) --- Arabic, "Athana." Syriac, "Ahmathane." The memoirs of Cyrus had probably been conveyed to Ecbatana, which was built by Dejoces, the first king of the Medes, and greatly enlarged by his successor, Phraortes. (Calmet) ---*Province.* Media now only formed a province of the empire. (Tirinus)

VERSE 3

And foundations is not found in Septuagint, Syriac, and Arabic, but it is in Chaldean. The temple was thus of larger dimensions than that of Solomon, which was only 30 cubits high, and 20 broad inside, 3 Kings vi. 2. The Rabbins assign 100 for each, (Tr. Middot. iv. 6.) speaking perhaps of the temple rebuilt by Herod, with still greater magnificence. Josephus allows 100 in height, and 60 in breadth. But the Scripture only speaks of 54 cubits breadeth, and 99 in length including the adjoining edifices. (Calmet) ---*Breadth,* from the front to the end of the holy of holies, which we should call the length. (Tirinus) --- This temple was lower than Solomon's by one half, (2 Paralipomenon iii. 4; Menochius) unless those 120 cubits refer only to a tower. (Haydock)

VERSE 4

Unpolished, to correspond with the polished stones and cedar employed by Solomon, 3 Kings vi. 36. (Menochius) --- Protestants, "great stones." See chap. v. 8. --- *Charges.* It appears that the Jews furnished money and meat to pay for the wood, chap. i. 4., and iii. 7. Some annual sum might be assigned by Cyrus, either for the building, or for the daily holocausts. (Calmet)

VERSE 5

Placed formerly, before the destruction of the temple. Protestants, "and place *them* in the house of God."

VERSE 8

Hindered. Thus Darius trod in the footsteps, or perhaps exceeded the liberality of Cyrus. (Haydock)

VERSE 9

Complaint. Protestants, "without fail," (Haydock) or "delay." (Montanus) (Calmet)

VERSE 11

Nailed. Protestants, "hanged." Septuagint, "covered with wounds, *or* fastened on it." (Haydock) --- Some think that the criminal was to be scourged. (De Dieu) --- "Let him be hanged on the wood, which shall stand upright, after his house shall have been demolished." (Vatable) --- Such was the custom of the Persians. (Grotius) --- Aman perished on the gallows, which he had erected in his own house for Mardocheus, Esther vii. 9. --- *Confiscated.* Protestants, "be made a dunghill for this." (Haydock) (Syriac, &c.) --- We find some examples of such a treatment, 4 Kings x. 27., and Daniel iii. 5., and ix. 6. The effects of those who were condemned to die, in Persia, were generally confiscated, Esther iii. 13, and viii 11, and ix. 14.

VERSE 14

Artaxerxes, one of the seven who overturned the power of the magi; (Usher, the year of the world 3483) or rather the king of Persia, who lived some time after this, and was very favorable to the Jews. He sent Esdras (the year of the world 3537) and Nehemias (the year of the world 3550) with great powers into the country. (Calmet)

VERSE 15

Adar, corresponding with our February and March. (Menochius) --- In the latter month they celebrated the Passover, ver. 19. --- *Darius.* Hence twenty years had elapsed from the first foundation. They might continue to embellish the temple other twenty-seven years, as the Jews assert; (John ii. 20) unless they speak of the repairs made by Herod, (Baronius; Tirinus) or exaggerate, (Grotius) being under a mistake. (Salien, the year of the world 3537.)

VERSE 17

Goats, which had not left off sucking. (Menochius) (Numbers vii. 87.) --- *Israel.* The Samaritan Chronicles assert that the tribes returned, as the prophets had foretold, and the sacred history seems to suppose (Calmet) which may be true of many, (Haydock) though the greatest part remained in captivity. (Calmet)

VERSE 18

Moses. (Numbers iii. 8.) David had perfected the plan, 1 Paralipomenon xxiii., &c. (Haydock)

VERSE 19

And. Here the author resumes the Hebrew language. (Calmet) --- *Captivity,* from which they were released, ver. 17. (Haydock)

VERSE 20

One man, with zeal and unanimity; so that a second Phase was not to be celebrated, 2 Paralipomenon xxx. 3.

VERSE 21

To them, becoming proselytes, and receiving circumcision, Exodus xii. 48.

VERSE 22

Assyria. The successors of Cyrus now ruled over those countries, (Calmet) which had belonged to the most potent Assyrian and Chaldean monarchs; and therefore the titles are given to them indiscriminately. (Tirinus)

CHAPTER VII

VERSE 1

Things, sixty-eight years after the journey of Zorobabel. (Calmet) --- Salien adds ten years more. (Haydock) --- *Artaxerxes* Longimanus. (Menochius) (Tirinus) --- *Son,* or great grandson *of Saraias,* who had been slain 121 years. Esdras was still living, in the days of Nehemias. Many persons are omitted in this genealogy. The immediate descendants of Azarias may be found, 1 Paralipomenon vi. Similarity of names has occasioned many mistakes. 3 Esdras viii. reckons only eleven persons between Aaron and Esdras; and 4 Esdras i. has eighteen; whereas here we behold sixteen generations, and [in] 1 Paralipomenon, twenty-two. (Calmet)

VERSE 5

Beginning of the Jewish republic.

VERSE 6

Went up, a second time, 2 Esdras xii. 1. (Worthington) --- *Ready.* Hebrew *mahir,* "diligent," &c. (Haydock) --- *Scribe,* not so much noted for his skill in writing fast, or drawing up deeds, as for his knowledge of the divine law. (Calmet) --- The gospel sometimes gives the title of *scribe* to the doctors of the law, Matthew xxii. 35., with Mark xii. 28. It is peculiarly due to Esdras, who gave a correct copy of the Scriptures, and wrote them in a different character, leaving the ancient one to the Samaritans, that the people might be less connected. (Bellarmine, De Verb. xx. 1, citing (Tirinus) the most learned Fathers and Jewish writers. (Calmet, Diss.) --- The author of 4 Esdras (xiv. 19) intimates that the sacred books had been all destroyed, and were dictated again to Esdras by the Holy Spirit. But this book is not of sufficient authority to establish so dangerous an opinion; (Haydock) which is refuted by the whole context of the Bible, in which we see that the law was never forgotten. (Calmet, Diss.) (Du Hamel) --- As Esdras was inspired, what additions he might make, must be accounted divine and authentic. (Calmet) --- *Hand;* protection, (Delrio, adag. 217,) or inspiration. (Menochius) --- God can incline the heart of the king, (Proverbs xxi.) to accomplish his decrees. (Haydock)

VERSE 9

Month. Thus four entire months were spent on the journey, as they did not go the shortest way, and had much baggage, &c. (Calmet)

VERSE 10

Heart. Thinking continually (Menochius) how he might keep the law himself, and direct others. (Haydock) --- It would be well if all would thus teach by example, like Jesus Christ, who *began to do* and then *to teach.* (Haydock) --- *Judgment.* Both these terms express the same thing. (Menochius)

VERSE 11

Of the edict, is a farther explanation of the *letter.* (Haydock)

VERSE 12

Kings. This title was placed on the tomb of Cyrus, (Strabo xv.) and denoted a very powerful king. Artaxerxes had many tributaries in Media, Sidon, &c. The kings of Assyria had before assumed such pompous titles, Osee viii. 10. (Calmet) --- *The most learned,* comes later in the original Chaldean. (Haydock) --- "The priest, scribe of the law, perfection, (health and happiness, (Calmet) or *consummate* in learning, &c.; Haydock) as at present." (Calmet) --- *Gemir uceheneth,* "perfection (Castel. Lexic.) even now," chap. iv. 10. Protestants, "perfect *peace,* and at such a time." (Haydock)

VERSE 14

Counselors. Interpreters of the laws. (Josephus, [Antiquities] xi. 6.) --- The number seems to have been established at the courts of the Assyrian and Chaldean monarchs, Tobias xii. 15. We find their names, Esther i. 10, 14. The history of this queen happened in the reign of Darius Hystaspes. (Calmet) --- *Hand.* By this he was to pass sentence, ver. 25. (Haydock) --- The Jews were authorized to follow their own laws (Calmet) under the Persian dominion, ver. 26. (Tirinus)

VERSE 16

Babylon, which the Chaldeans may freely give. (Menochius)

VERSE 20

By me. Hebrew, "to spend, take it out of the king's treasure-house." Septuagint adds, "and from me."

VERSE 22

Salt was used in all the sacrifices, Leviticus ii. 13. In 3 Esdras no mention is made of oil or salt; but we read, "and all other things in abundance."

VERSE 24

Nathinites. 3 Esdras, "sacred slaves." (Haydock) --- Artaxerxes confirms the immunities granted by the law of God, (Numbers iii. 6, 12) by the kings of Egypt, (Genesis xlvii. 22) and by all nations to the ministers of religion. (Calmet)

VERSE 25

River. 3 Esdras, "In all Syria and Phoenicia." (Haydock) --- Hitherto, it seems, the royal judges had decided all affairs of consequence, which required any public chastisement.

VERSE 26

Banishment. Hebrew literally, "eradication" by death or exile, (Calmet) or by being cut off from all society, chap. x. 8. (De Dieu) --- Septuagint, "correction." (Haydock)

VERSE 27

Blessed. Here the author beings to write again in Hebrew and in the following verse, Esdras speaks in [the first] person. (Calmet)

CHAPTER VIII

VERSE 2

Hattus. He was of the royal family, (Haydock) as the former were descendants of the two sons of Aaron. (Calmet) --- The great numbers which were persuaded to return from Babylon, signify the conversions made by holy preachers. (Ven. Bede) (Worthington)

VERSE 5

Sons. Septuagint and Arabic add, "of Zathoe, Sechenias, the son of Aziel." The Syriac supplies the name of "Gabo, the son of Nahzael," which seems to have been lost. (Calmet) --- Junius translates, "of the descendants Sechenias N. son of Jahaziel."

VERSE 10

Sons of. Septuagint supply "Baani," whose name occurs, chap. ii. 10, and is here visibly wanting. (Calmet)

VERSE 13

Last. Coming after their brethren, chap. ii. 13.

VERSE 14

Zachur. Hebrew and Septuagint, "Zabud." (Calmet) --- Two letters have been mistaken. (Haydock)

VERSE 15

Ahava. This river (ver. 21, and 31) runs through the territory of the same name, called Hava; (4 Kings xvii. 24) the people of which exchanged places with the Israelites. Esdras makes a circuit to prevail on some of the latter to return with him, unless he began his journey from Susa. Babylon comprises all that country. (Calmet) --- *None there,* who were not priests, ver. 2. (Lyranus) (Menochius)

VERSE 16

Sent. Septuagint, "&c.," "to Eliezer," &c., in order to give them his orders what to say to Eddo, who presided at Chasphia, as the sequel shows. --- *Wise men,* instructors of the people, (2 Paralipomenon xxxv. 3; Calmet) Levites. (Menochius)

VERSE 17

Chasphia. The Caspian mountains, between Media and Hyrcania. Here the Nathinites were forced to labor, under Eddo. The service of the temple would be far more eligible. (Calmet)

VERSE 21

Fast it seems for eight days, so that they departed on the 12th, ver. 31. (Menochius) --- It will not suffice to leave sin, we must also do works of satisfaction. (Worthington)

VERSE 22

Forsake him. Apostates are treated with the greatest severity. (Menochius) --- Esdras thought that the glory of God was at stake, and he would not show any diffidence in Providence, or scandalize the infidels. (Calmet) --- We ought not to ask princes for what we should despise. (Du Hamel)

VERSE 26

A hundred. Hebrew adds, "talents," *vessels of silver.* (Haydock) --- Some Rabbins suppose there were only 100, each of this weight, which is not probable. All the silver vessels, of different sizes, weighed 100 talents. There was the same quantity of golden vessels. (Calmet)

VERSE 27

Solids. Hebrew *adarconim.* Darics, equivalent to the golden sicle. (Calmet) (1 Paralipomenon xxix. 7.) ---*Best.* Protestants, "of fine copper, precious as gold." It might resemble the Corinthian brass, or *aurichalcum,* (Haydock) composed of gold, silver, and brass melted together, in the burning of Corinth, by L. Mummius. (Pliny, [Natural History] xxxiv. 2.) --- Yet no such Corinthian vessels have come down to us; so that the account seems fabulous; and, at any rate, the city was not taken in the days of Esdras, but in the year 608 of Rome. We cannot say whether he speaks of copper, brass, &c. (Calmet)

VERSE 35

Israel. Some of the different tribes certainly returned, chap. vi. 17.

VERSE 36

Lords, (satrapis.) 3 Esdras, "to the royal officers and governors of Cœlosyria and Phoenicia; and they glorified," &c. *Furthered,* by their assistance (Haydock) and praise. They formed their sentiments, as is usual, by those of the king. (Calmet)

CHAPTER IX

VERSE 1

Abominations, or sins, (Menochius) marrying with infidels, contrary to the law, Exodus xxxiv. 15., and Deuteronomy vii. 3. (Du Hamel) --- Malachy [Malachias] (ii. 11.) reprehends this conduct, and threatens both rulers and people who tolerate it, with God's indignation. (Worthington)

VERSE 2

First. Or "was in this first transgression," incurred by those who returned with Zorobabel; or "was concerned in this very heinous transgression;" *in transgressione hac prima.* (Calmet) --- Protestants, "hath been chief." 3 Esdras, "and the leaders and grandees partook in this illegal affair, from its commencement." Septuagint, "and the hand of the chiefs was in this transgress, in the beginning." This would greatly increase the difficulty of reformation. Some of the princes were however ready to undertake the work, and had preserved themselves from the two general contagion. (Haydock) --- All marriages with the Moabites, &c., were prohibited, if the women remained infidels, Exodus xxxiv. (Tirinus)

VERSE 3

Coat, (*tunicam*) or inner garment. (Haydock) --- *Mourning.* Hebrew, "astonished." (Syriac) (Montanus) (Calmet) (Protestants) --- Septuagint, "alone." 3 Esdras, "pensive and in grief." (Haydock) --- Arabic, "not uttering a word." See Job i. 20, and ii. 8. This was the ordinary posture of people in sorrow, Isaias iii. 26. (Calmet)

VERSE 4

To me, in the court of the temple, chap. x. 1. (Menochius) --- *Sacrifice,* which was offered last of all, about sun-set, Exodus xxix. 38. The Jews commonly protract their fasts till the stars appear. (Leo, p 3, art 8.)

VERSE 7

At this day. Notwithstanding the favorable decrees of Cyrus, &c., the greatest part of the people continued in captivity, being dispersed, some into Egypt, others into distant countries, beyond the Euphrates. (Calmet)

VERSE 8

As a. Protestants, "for a little space, grace hath been *showed* from the Lord," (Haydock) and yet we are again irritating Him! (Calmet) --- *A pin,* or *nail,* here signifies a small settlement or holding; which Esdras begs for, to preserve even a part of the people, who, by their great iniquity, had incurred the anger of God. (Challoner) --- Allusion is made to the pins which fasten down a tent, (Isaias xxxiii. 20., and liv. 2) or hinder a ship from being carried from the shore, (Tigurin; Menochius) on which utensils are hung up, (Tournemine) referring to the magistrates, who were now of the same country. (Tirinus) (Isaias xxii. 21.) (Delrio, adag. 218.) --- Septuagint, "a support." Hebrew *yathed,* denotes also a walking-stick, nail, &c. (Menochius) --- *Eyes,* fill us with joy, in perfect security. --- *Little life,* free us from danger. (Calmet) --- Esdras is afraid to ask for the impunity of all, but only begs that a small part may be spared, like a nail or post from a house, which may serve to rebuild it. (Worthington)

VERSE 9

Fence. Hebrew *gader,* "the name which the Carthaginians" gave to Cadiz, "as it signifies a fence," or an inclosure. (Pliny, [Natural History] xxii.) (Calmet) --- Some Latin manuscripts read *spem,* "hope." (Lyranus) --- The Tigurin version understands the wall of Jerusalem, built in a hurry. (Menochius) --- But this was not perfected, (Haydock) if begun, till the time of Nehemias, 2 Esdras i. 3. (Calmet) --- God gave his protection to the people, (Haydock; Delrio, adag. 219.) by the king of Persia. (Tirinus)

VERSE 11

Mouth, like a vessel brim-full. (Menochius) --- Protestants, "from one end ot the other." (Haydock)

VERSE 12

Peace. Alliance, (Menochius) or advantage. See Psalm cxxi. 8. Moses had thus proscribed the Moabites, &c., as he had done the people of Chanaan still more severely. The Israelites were to execute God's decrees, Deuteronomy xxiii. 6. (Calmet) --- The obstinate idolaters were to be exterminated.

VERSE 13

Saved us. Protestants, "hast punished us less than our iniquities *deserve* and hast given us such deliverance as this." Septuagint, "hast made our transgressions light," (Haydock) not weighing them with rigid severity. (Calmet)

VERSE 14

That. Hebrew, "should we again break, &c. Wouldst thou not be angry?" &c.

VERSE 15

To be saved from our iniquities, which are still upon us. (Haydock) --- We confess that, if we should be treated according to our deserts, we could expect no redress. But we trust in thy mercies, which have hitherto supported and brought us back from slavery. (Calmet)

CHAPTER X

VERSE 1

God, in the court of the people, before the eastern gate.

VERSE 2

Sechenias. 3 Esdras calls him "Jechoias." See chap. viii. 5. The name of Sechenias is not found among the transgressors; (ver. 20.) but that of Jehiel is, ver. 26. It seems, however, that the former returned with Esdras, and speaks in the name of the people, to encourage them to confess their guilt, (Calmet) unless his name be omitted. (Menochius) --- *Repentance.* Hebrew, "yet there is hope, (Protestants) *or* an assembly of Israel." (Du Dieu)

VERSE 3

Covenant. The marrying with strange women seemed to have annulled the covenant of God. --- *Of them.* The children were to follow the mothers, as in other unlawful connections. Their being suffered to remain behind, might have had dangerous consequences. (Calmet) --- The custom of divorcing was then in force, (Tirinus) and the Jews looked upon all as null, which was done contrary to the law; (Ven. Bede; Estius; Calmet; Grotius) though here the law was only prohibitory. (Cajetan) (Tirinus) --- As all was directed by the will of God, the dictates of humanity would not be disregarded (Calmet) on this trying occasion. (Haydock) --- The children might be placed in houses for education. (Cajetan) (Tirinus)

VERSE 4

Thy part. The high priest not acting, (Menochius) Esdras was appointed chief, (Haydock) and his abilities were universally acknowledged. (Calmet)

VERSE 6

Before. 3 Esdras, "the court *or* hall of the temple." (Haydock) --- *Eliasib.* His son and successor is styled Joiada, 2 Esdras xii. 10. The same person had often many names, (Calmet) or Johanan might be a younger son. (Menochius) --- Josephus ([Antiquities] xi. 5.) says, that Esdras went to the apartments of John and Eliasib. (Haydock) --- Esdras, though sent extraordinarily by God, repairs to the son of the priest, as St. Paul conferred with other apostles, Galatians ii. (Worthington)

VERSE 8

Away. Hebrew and Septuagint, "subjected to anathema," (Calmet) and utterly destroyed; (Haydock) or, according to some editions of the Septuagint and Josephus, "consecrated to the temple." Esdras exercised the power which had been entrusted to him, chap. vii. 16.

VERSE 9

Ninth. Casleu, (Zacharias vii. 1.) which corresponds with our November and December. (Menochius) ---*Street.* Court, which afforded as yet no shelter from the rain. (Calmet) --- This would tend to punish them for their sin, and to make them more sensible to it. (Worthington)

VERSE 11

Confession. Septuagint, "give praise;" which is done by repentance and virtue. (Menochius) --- Confess your faults, and submit to the justice of God, Josue vii. 19. (Calmet)

VERSE 14

Cities. It is not clear whether the rulers went to the different cities, or the principal men of each gave information, and caused the guilty to appear before Esdras, at Jerusalem. (Haydock)

VERSE 16

So. Cajetan improperly concludes, that the sentence was not put in execution; because Nehemias (chap. xiii. 23) complains of such marriages. (Calmet) --- But the guilty might have resumed their women. (Haydock) --- *Went.* Hebrew, "were separated." (Haydock) --- By making a small change, we may translate, with 3 Esdras, "and Esdras separated *or* chose the men." Josephus seems generally to have followed the Greek of 3 Esdras. The Syriac says there were 20 judges.

VERSE 19

Hands. Thus the Persians confirmed their most solemn engagements. (Calmet)

VERSE 25

Israel. Laymen, (Calmet) not of the tribe of Levi. (Menochius)

VERSE 30

Moab. The inhabitants of this town, as well as of *Nebo,* (ver. 43.) are specified.

VERSE 44

Children. Hebrew may be, "and some of these women had exposed their children." But most follow the Septuagint and Vulgate. 3 Esdras ix. 36, "and they ejected them with their children." None was spared. (Calmet) --- One great inconvenience of such connections is, that the offspring is illegitimate. (Worthington) --- Only 17 priests, 10 Levites, and 86 laymen, are stigmatized as guilty of this scandal; yet these fill Israel with confusion, and Esdras with extreme affliction. (Haydock)

Made in the USA
Columbia, SC
16 February 2022